Desert Awakenings

NorthWord Press
5900 Green Oak Drive
Minnetonka, MN 55343
1-800-328-3895

Book design by Russell S. Kuepper

Library of Congress Cataloging-in-Publication Data

Murray, John A.

   Desert awakenings / John A. Murray ; photography by Jeff Gnass.

     p. cm.

     Includes bibliographical references (p.   ).

     ISBN 1-55971-666-5 (hardcover)

  1. Southwest, New--Pictorial works. 2. Southwest, New--Description and travel. 3. Deserts--Southwest, New--Pictorial works. 4. Mexico, North--Pictorial works. 5. Mexico, North--Description and travel. 6. Deserts--Mexico, North--Pictorial works. 7. Murray, John A. --Journeys--Southwest, New.

  I. Gnass, Jeff. II. Title.

  F787.M87 1998   98-3418

  979--dc21

Printed in China
02 01 00 99 98 / 5 4 3 2 1

Desert Awakenings

By John A. Murray
Photography by Jeff Gnass

NorthWord Press
Minnetonka, Minnesota

Santa Rosa Range, Nevada.

CONTENTS

We have had a spectacular and dangerous trip. All went well through Death Valley, Boulder Dam, Zion, North Rim, South Rim. Then we spent the night on Walpi Mesa, proceeded to Chinle and had two spectacular, stormy days at Canyon de Chelly. I photographed the White House Ruins from almost the identical spot of the O'Sullivan picture! Can't wait until I see what I got.

—Ansel Adams
Letter to Beaumont and Nancy Newhall, October 26, 1941

Preface

In an essay entitled "The Wisdom of the Desert," the Trappist monk and poet Thomas Merton writes of the desert as a realm of spiritual inspiration. He recounts the history of the Christian mystics of the fourth century A.D. and their quest for knowledge and truth in the deserts of Egypt and Palestine. Like the Indian Yogis or the Tibetan monks, these individuals sought to cross the canyon that separates who we are from what we are, and comprehend the ultimate nature of reality. For ages the deserts of the world were seen, alternately, as a spare, disciplined landscape providing opportunities for solitude and revelation, or as a forsaken emptiness

Above: Spider Rock, Canyon de Chelly National Monument, Arizona.
Right: Sunrise at Maricopa Point, Grand Canyon National Park, Arizona.

into which well-armed legions periodically marched and disappeared. Deserts—from the Latin *desertus*, meaning abandoned—were equated with the absence of life in both a literal and a figurative sense.

In our time a quiet change has occurred. The human race has begun to look at deserts in a third way—as a place for the aesthetic appreciation of nature, as well as for physical exercise and recreation. Deserts are no longer the exclusive domain of prophets and outlaws. They are seen as not only having life, but as having an abundance of life, often in quite fantastic forms. As a result of this change in perspective, there has been a major structural change in the way society relates to deserts. Preservation is now pursued as vigorously as irrigation projects and mineral exploitation were in previous eras. Beginning with Grand Canyon National Monument in 1908, the United States became the first country in history to establish national parks in deserts, and, as a people, we became the first to regularly seek them out as refuges from civilization. Now, countries around the world, from Israel to

Australia, are following suit and establishing parks in desert regions for the benefit of their populations.

Some of the most beautiful places on earth are found in the deserts of North America. It has been my good fortune over the past twenty years, and that of my friend Jeff Gnass as well, to visit many of these locations. Some of those that immediately come to mind include the view from Muley Point in southern Utah, looking out over the "Goosenecks" of the San Juan River and across Monument Valley; the panorama at virtually any point from the Puerto Blanco Road in Organ Pipe Cactus National Monument, looking north toward Kino Peak or south into the desert mountains of Mexico; or the scenery along State Route 178 in Death Valley, which takes in Badwater Basin, the lowest point in North America (-282 feet), as well as Telescope Peak (11,049 feet), all in one sweep of color and form.

Quite often, the more intimate trailside alcoves are just as compelling. A 400-million-year-old trilobite fossil, imbedded in a limestone ledge and surrounded by the yellow blossoms of a prickly pear cactus, can command the attention as fully as

Preface

the Grand Canyon at one's back. Similarly, a humble creosote bush, tenaciously growing in an alkaline basin in southern New Mexico, can inspire as much admiration as a multi-branched saguaro cactus standing fifty feet tall in a less heroic situation. In this book Jeff and I share some of these special places with you, through words and images. We have at all times kept in mind Leonardo da Vinci's statement in his *Treatise on Painting*: "Painting is poetry that is seen rather than felt, and poetry is painting that is felt rather than seen." In an age of photography and belles lettres, this formulation seems particularly relevant, though in a way perhaps even da Vinci's active imagination would not have anticipated.

The scientists tell us that a quartz crystal in its symmetry reveals the atomic structure of matter. In the same way do our acts of love, however small and seemingly insignificant, present an outward manifestation of ultimate nature. One could sit alone in the desert for thirty years, as with Thomas Merton's hermits, and probably advance no further toward that elusive final truth.

Love them, dear readers, these lost and lonely lands, and you will find that in the end what you get back is equal to what you give.

CHAPTER ONE

To him who in the love of nature holds
Communion with her visible forms, she speaks
A various language.

—William Cullen Bryant, "Thanatopsis"

Mojave Desert

WILD PALMS

The heat was gathering. The air was still. It was that time of day in the desert when shadows disappear and the local star reveals its legendary strength. Life goes underground. Hops, crawls, slithers, or burrows down a familiar tunnel and finds a dark, somewhat humid chamber in which to sleep. The quiet above ground becomes as immense as the emptiness of the sky. Nothing moves, except a solitary turkey vulture, idly circling on a thermal. The sensitive skin on the top of the ears, the tip of the nose, and other regions left uncovered begin

Above: Joshua tree limb and threadleaf groundsel, Mojave National Preserve, California.
Right: Southwest Palm Grove, Anza-Borrego Desert State Park, California.

Globemallow and barrel cactus in New York Mountains, Mojave National Preserve, California.

to redden. Somewhere in the inscrutable recesses of the brain these sensations, and others, are duly registered as developments not to be ignored.

My feet on the hot sand made a steady crunching, and when I stopped walking the silence was enough to hasten the general pace of the journey. Where was I headed? An oasis in the Mojave. I had started the hike late in the morning and was about halfway to my destination. The oasis was reported to have a fine grove of native fan palms, one of the loveliest in southern California.

After climbing the third rise, I stood on a level divide between two broad drainages. To the south was the northern edge of the Colorado Desert,

Joshua tree—
Joshua Tree National Park, California.

a much lower and drier desert. To the west were ancient stone hills. If you looked at them long enough, in the vibrating shimmer of heat, they became enormous desert tortoises. You could see the wrinkled necks, the antiquarianlike eyes, the bulky weathered shells, the clawed reptilian feet straining to break free of the earth. You blinked and the mirage lost its effect. Somewhere to the east, in a wilderness of rocks, was my destination, a meandering granitic canyon. At the bottom of the canyon flowed that most rare of desert commodities: a steady trickle of water.

As I hiked along I considered many things: the trail before me, the spring flowers beside the trail, the amount of water in the pack, the

Sandstone formations at Bowl of Fire, Lake Mead National Recreation Area, Nevada.

Death Valley phacelia and sandstone outcroppings, Valley of Fire State Park, Nevada.

number of hours remaining in the day. Every half mile or so I turned and surveyed the desiccated country behind me, noting the position of what were becoming increasingly familiar landforms. A small but distinct knob of rocks topped a faraway ridge. If I aimed for that, even if I lost the trail, I would find my way back to the end of the road. Maps are excellent aids for the backcountry traveler, but sometimes, in the rush to get underway, they are forgotten.

I took particular note of the wildflowers beside the trail, because it had been a wet winter. In the Mojave, if nowhere else, the record-breaking precipitation was a blessing. The desert wore a light chemise of green. Where the slopes faced south and the seeds had been generously watered, the flower displays were spectacular: watermelon red beavertail cactus, alpenglow purple hedgehog cactus, sulphur yellow barrel cactus, and many others. All year long the desert plants saved for this. Absorbed miserly rains. Hoarded moisture in tightly packed cells. Guarded precious buds with barbed spines. This was their Mardi Gras, their Fiesta, their Carnival. Their rite of spring.

Beavertail cactus,
Joshua Tree National Park, California.

Branching phacelia and Mojave yucca,
Joshua Tree National Park, California.

Van Gogh would have loved it, splashed vibrant colors all over the canvas, probably gotten a really bad sunburn with that red hair and freckled skin of his, madly searched his case of oils for a blood-red pigment to paint the scarlet blossoms of the claret cup cactus.

The cactus blossoms were nice, but the most striking wildflowers favored the Mojave yuccas. Beneath nearly every yucca was a thick bed of golden Mexican poppies and lavender-blue lupine. From the mixed blossoms, subtle fragrances lured all manner of butterflies. There were tiger swallowtails and wayward orange and black monarchs and some sort of local checkerspot I had never seen before. When they sank their antennaed heads into the center of the petals the gaudily painted wings stopped moving for one brief, delicious moment. The ultimate sugar junkies. The yuccas were also heavily flowered. Each stalk bore a cluster of blossoms with petals the color of white candle wax. I puzzled a long time over the close association and finally concluded that visiting songbirds must disperse wildflower seeds around the yuccas.

As I hiked through the rugged rocky uplands there were scattered Joshua trees. Not as many as in the Queen's Valley or on Cima Dome, but still a good number. These trees are either grotesque or exquisite, depending on your point of view. In 1844 western explorer John C. Fremont called the Joshua tree "the most repulsive tree in the vegetable kingdom." A few years later the Mormons passed through. They thought the uplifted branches were like the arms of Joshua beckoning them to the promised land, hence the name. People have been arguing ever since.

I stopped in front of a two- or three-hundred-year-old tree. It was an odd-looking plant, no doubt about that. My first impression was of top-heaviness. The trunk was small, only about twenty inches in diameter, and the numerous branches were stout and forking. At the end of each branch were heavy daggerlike leaves. Because this was spring, there were also ivory blossom clusters similar to those on their cousins, the yucca. These caused the ponderous branches to droop. As far as I'm concerned, Joshua trees are a masterpiece of concision and adaptation. Without them, the Mojave would be like the Colorado Rockies without aspen, the streets of New York without Italian ice vendors, the halls of Congress without lobbyists. In a sense, Joshua trees *are* the Mojave. And in 1994 this lovely palm oasis and 792,000 acres around it was set aside as Joshua Tree National Park.

An hour later, standing at the prow of a hill, I was afforded a view of the country ahead. The landscape was, in a word, bleak. Here was the Earth before the Cambrian explosion assembled fish and ferns from amoebas and blue-green algae, or, ages hence, after the sun has gone supernova and deep-fried the first three planets. Rocks, rocks, and more rocks. Hulking mountains partially buried in their own rubble, deep canyons with fossil streams, massive boulders the size of ten-story buildings, wind-blasted plateaus, weird basaltic labyrinths, huge eroded buttresses, shattered rock plains.

Plants were so hard-pressed for soil in this region they

Cliffrose and Joshua tree forest, Mojave National Preserve, California.

Joshua trees and Bigelow's coreopsis, Horse Canyon Wilderness, California.

Castle Peaks, Mojave National Preserve, California.

squeezed from rock fissures, somehow finding nourishment in the dust and decayed matter at the bottom of the gap. Some were beautiful, like the skinny ocotillo, with tiny bursts of red flowers like exploding Roman candles. Others were not, like the spiny cholla, which is what a porcupine would be if it were a plant.

The scene evoked another desolate image—the Valley of the Dead in Egypt. Walk in the Mojave for a day and you can understand why the pharaohs worshipped the sun. The sun was the controlling reality of their desert world, just as it is in the deserts of southern California.

The trail switchbacked into the abyss and several hundred feet later brought me to the edge of what would elsewhere be a stream. Here there was only sand. In the sand you could see where the current had previously flowed, for the water had sculpted channels and braids and riffles, and you could almost imagine the sand flowing along as a liquid. In fact, if you stared at it long enough, in the heat, the sand began to move. Turn away, look back, and the illusion vanished.

Mesquite Flat, Death Valley National Park, California.

Where the sand was heavy and coarse it formed dark edges and some of the patterns were beautiful, radiating concentrically around a sculpted stone or delicately paralleling a cutback. Where the sand was fine and lighter-colored, it spread out thickly, as on a beach. When examined closely the sand was discovered to be diverse—bits of clear quartz and shiny mica and reddish feldspar and darker volcanic minerals I could not identify. A prospector would know how to read the sand. So would a horned toad hunting for scarab beetles.

There were little worlds in the streambed. Anthills that would become busy under the stars. Dark holes housing reclusive tarantulas. Inch-high flower beds of white fleabane that would require a thick hand lens to peruse.

I widened my search, struck out upstream for a wide stretch where a side trail crossed the dry watercourse. Here, tracks—black-tailed deer and coyotes and kangaroo rats—were all mingled together in evidence of the local nightlife. Just how the indigents managed their affairs in such a landscape I do not know. But their tracks indeed

Sand dunes at Mesquite Flat, Death Valley National Park, California.

confirmed their existence. It occurred to me that a whole book could be written on sand. Not just sand, but the stretch of sand in this dry watercourse. The sand was a book in which was written the story of the desert.

I followed the sand upstream, thinking I was on the trail, intently reading the tracks, trying to acquire some sense of the neighborhood. A quarter mile farther on, a ten-foot wall of quartz monzonite blocked the way. There was a smooth lip over which flash floods had poured for half a million years. Below it was a splash basin where the periodic thundering water had hollowed out the bedrock. Clearly this was not the trail. I retraced my steps.

Sandpaper plants and Wallace eriophyllums, Joshua Tree National Park, California.

The trail to the oasis angled up the other side of the canyon, crossed another tedious pile of rocks, descended another canyon, angled its way through sandy subterranean corridors, climbed a second canyon wall, and then repeated the whole process again. This happened two more times. I didn't mind, even if I was half lost in the middle of the Mojave. I'd known worse. In the Mojave, even at the bottom of a nameless canyon, it was a nice summer day.

Nature writers have flocked to the desert in numbers out of all proportion to the size of the region. Elsewhere, the literary situation is not nearly so robust, especially in the Old South and the Midwest. Why is that? What is it about the desert provinces that most attracts

Joshua tree forest at Lee Flat, Death Valley National Park, California.

Desert mallow and sandstone, Valley of Fire State Park, Nevada.

nature writers? The vastness? The life forms? The mild winters? The public lands? The peace and quiet? The aesthetic clarity? I would guess the last—the desert is, for any artist, pure inspiration.

On and on I trudged, through a maze of narrow passageways with perpendicular walls. On and on, through canyons measureless to man. Finally I began to encounter foot-long black-collared lizards. Not just one or two lizards, but five or six, and this, I surmised, was a good sign. Where animals have the energy to hold a mini-convention at midday, there must be water. If only they could talk and tell me how near I was. My pace quickened. Finally the trail took me up the side of another canyon wall. I sensed this was the last, or had to be the last, and I was right.

At the top I caught my breath, stood fully upright and saw a colony of ten or eleven California fan palms perched high in the rocks of an opposing canyon wall. A few quick steps through some medicinal-smelling creosote brought me to the rim of the famous secret barranca. It was filled a quarter of the way with a fertile oasis of California fan

Spreading fleabane daisies and juniper wood,
Virgin Mountains, Nevada.

Creosote bushes at Kelso Dunes,
Mojave National Preserve, California.

palms. The sight of palm trees, not mirages but real palm trees, after walking half the day in a half-baked desert, was immensely restorative.

There was a gentle breeze in the bright green canyon, and the palm fronds swayed slightly, making a pleasant, peaceful rustling sound. And from the shadows underneath the palms came the welcome sound of moving water and the cheerful song of the canyon wren: *zzzzeeeep, zzzzeeeep, tee-tee-tee-tee-tee-tee-teer-teer.*

I listened for a moment, absorbing the music and the scene, realizing I had indeed come to a special place. There was life here. Lots of it. Hundreds of square miles of desert and here was a piece of something different. Greater biodiversity, some would say. More poetry, I would say.

Four switchbacks brought me to the canyon floor. Bighorn sheep tracks prominently marked the sand. They were squarish, blocky tracks, several sizes larger than the slender cloven tracks of deer. A good-sized herd called this place home, and some of the rams were big. Down their ancient trail, a trail wide enough for sheep, I walked. Beside the trail ran a stream. At times it was three inches deep, flowing over a cool bed of sparkling sand. At other times it hurried over a ledge and filled a clear pool two feet deep. No pupfish, though. Too alkaline and isolated for that. The splashing water sparkled on the trunks of the palms and there were whiptail lizards scampering up and down the trunks. Farther back in places I could not see were scorpions and centipedes, Gila monsters and pit vipers. The well-armed creatures of the night.

All the while, the canyon wrens sang: *zzzeeep, zzzeeep, tee-tee-tee-tee-tee-teer-teer.* Occasionally I would see one of them, slender and rust-colored,

Sandstone formation,
Valley of Fire State Park, Nevada.

darting among the palms. Just when I fixed on the long pointed beak, the white throat, the backswept wings, the bird would disappear into the shadows. The canyon wrens were shy and kept to themselves. Only once, exploring the network of sheep trails, did I spot a nest. It was high in the rocks and was constructed of mud and twigs. The parents, like all parents, were preoccupied with the incessant demands of their offspring. What I loved most about the canyon wren was its song, which descended quickly through a series of notes like water falling from ledge to ledge in a little oasis stream.

My reconnaissance of the oasis was complete in an hour. It was about the size of a forty- or fifty-acre arbore-

Mosaic of desert wildflowers, Owens Peak Wilderness, California.

Broad gila and Joshua trees, Owens Peak Wilderness, California.

California poppies, owl clover, and goldfields, Antelope Valley California Poppy Reserve, California.

Twinpod, Red Rock Canyon Recreation Lands, Nevada.

tum. It extended only as far as the water ran. At the upper end, among a cluster of palms, the water poured from an underground spring. The stream ran through the grove for a third of a mile and then sank into the rocks as abruptly as it had appeared. All along the banks, in a narrow band, grew a dense subtropical jungle of grass, rushes, mesquite, jojoba, creosote, milkweed, willow, palo verde, and California fan palm.

The most interesting plant in the oasis was the palm, the only palm native to the western United States. Mature palms stood sixty feet tall, with a crown of five-foot palm fronds. The sturdy trunks were deeply weathered, with vertical cracks and fissures, and if you looked closely you could see

Porcupine prickly pear cactus,
Mojave National Preserve, California.

horizontal growth lines. As the palm fronds died they collapsed downward on the trunk. On a few of the trees these dead brown leaves formed a thick "skirt" that reached nearly to the ground. On most trees, for whatever reason, the skirts were practically nonexistent, and an energetic twelve-year-old could have climbed the trunk all the way to the top.

There were many nice views of the palms, but the best was on my back, looking upward. This was the view of the desert tortoise, or the coyote. From that perspective I could fully appreciate the pillarlike stature of the tree, the exotic richness of the crown, the symmetry of the split fronds against the sky. The fronds were really quite amazing.

Each leaf was long and sharp and deeply channeled. The surface was slightly varnished. The result was that they partially reflected light, a shimmering mirrorlike effect that was multiplied whenever a breeze stirred.

After the reconnaissance was complete and my field and sketch notebooks were put away I found a flat piece of 700-million-year-old gneiss above a pool and stripped off my sweaty shirt and lay down to sunbathe. Another nature writer hard at work.

I found a rock with some shade and took a nap. I fell asleep with a folded-over cotton shirt for a mattress and a rolled-up bandanna for a pillow. I guess I felt at home in the oasis. And why not? The human race has been living in oases ever since Olduvai Gorge, where we chipped obsidian edges and made palm-leaf shelters and subsisted on wild roots and palm fruit. When the siesta was over I took out my microcassette recorder, and taped a canyon wren. I let it run for a quarter of an hour, and the bird sang almost constantly in that time.

Whenever I turn the recording on now, and I often do before bed, it goes *zzzzeeeep, zzzzeeeep, tee-tee-tee-tee-tee-tee-teer-teer.* Over and over. Trickling water in the background. Light breezes in the palm fronds. The sound carries me back to a lovely canyon in the midst of the Mojave, a cool green place where a thousand years pass and nothing changes. A nation marches to war. A Great Depression ravages the land. A nation marches to war again. A generation of babies are born. Lives are lived. Cemeteries are slowly filled. Still the canyon wren sings, cheerfully, in a place the human race calls, for lack of a better word, the desert.

Bigelow's coreopsis and granite rocks,
Horse Canyon Wilderness, California.

CHAPTER TWO

First Born made the earth.
First Born made the earth.
Go along, go along, go along.
It's going along. Now all will remain as it is.

—Papago Song

Sonoran Desert

A WALK IN THE SUN

Approaching the Ajo Range from the west, on the dirt road off State Route 85 in south-western Arizona, I see a sharp mass of rocks rising abruptly from the surrounding country. The peaks are colored in thick red layers of lava alternating with light bands of tuff, or ash. Like all mountains of volcanic origin, the Ajo were born in fire. This is hard matter, highly resistant to erosion. One thinks of the accumulated slag at the bottom of the blacksmith's forge.

Above: Saguaro forest, Tucson Mountain Park, Arizona.
Right: Brittlebush and organ pipe cactus, Organ Pipe Cactus National Monument, Arizona.

Or the glassy supercompressed stone at the Trinity site. Or the adamantine views of a wilderness hermit. Or the tax code. Or the dense, turgid prose of a Supreme Court brief. These are rocks that only a prospector, a poet, or a landscape photographer could love.

The Ajo Range comprises the aesthetic heart of Organ Pipe Cactus National Monument, a 515-square-mile sanctuary that preserves a diverse sample of the Sonoran desert. Like several of our western parks and monuments, Organ Pipe was established in the late 1930s. Today Organ Pipe is one of our most popular national parks, especially in the winter, and is part of a modest conservation legacy that FDR's cousin

Theodore, who added 150 million acres to the inventory, would have approved of.

Two miles from the paved highway, the one-way track drops into a dry streambed—debris from the last flash flood scattered liberally on the banks—and then angles up the far side. The road straightens out. A brief respite before the really bad part certain to be waiting ahead. Every back road has its really bad part, especially every back road to anyplace worth seeing.

Gradually, the road winds across the bajada, or alluvial fan, toward the uplands. Mount Ajo (4,808 feet), rising without peer from the colossal train wreck of lower ridges, singularly

Brittlebush and owl clover in Puerto Blanco Mountains,
Organ Pipe Cactus National Monument, Arizona.

Organ pipe cactus, Organ Pipe Cactus National Monument, Arizona.

Brittlebush, cholla, and organ pipe cactus, Organ Pipe Cactus National Monument, Arizona.

Owl clover and saguaros in Puerto Blanco Mountains, Organ Pipe Cactus National Monument, Arizona.

Mexican poppies and cane cholla wood, Organ Pipe Cactus National Monument, Arizona.

Saguaro buds and blossoms,
Saguaro National Park, Arizona.

commands the attention of anyone looking up from the flatlands. It is a shattered hulk of a mountain, a ruined mass of rock, a grim porphyritic rampart that presents the appearance of having sustained a direct nuclear hit at some time in the recent past. The mountain, stripped of any aspect that could be called soft or gentle, is what the human heart would look like if it could be seen following one of those events we all dread—the loss of a loved one, the experience of war, the knowledge of impending death. In a single blinding flash everything is blasted away but the indestructible core.

It being spring, and spring after a particularly wet winter, the landscape is bright with color—cactus flowers such as are seen on the desert floor only about four or five times a century. I am tempted to stop, and savor the sweet calm and fleeting blossoms, and forgo any further serious plans, but I have an informal appointment with the highest peak in view. This is a mountain I have studied for years on topographic maps. I have driven a long way to make its acquaintance. And I am not inclined to be distracted. One climbs, or at least I climb, not to conquer but to be conquered, to be humbled, to be in the presence of an entity that invigorates and inspires even as it exhausts.

Four miles of sun-baked desert and wind-blown dust brings me to the entrance of Diablo Canyon. It was a favorite of the old people, the archaic ones who called these desert mountains home. Here, archaeologists have found their tools and flat grinding stones, the oldest dating to around 7,000 B.C. In more recent times, A.D. 150 to 1450, the Hohokam Indians camped in the canyon while on seasonal expeditions for mesquite beans and whitetail deer.

I am in the foothills now, Mount Ajo towering above to the height of a 300-story building. The road twists and turns through what ecologists call a mixed scrub community, an ancient peaceful society of brittlebush, creosote bush, and the various cacti—prickly pear, barrel, cholla, ocotillo, saguaro, and organ pipe. The last two are what make the Sonoran Desert distinctive. It is our only arboreal desert. Here, and here alone, are cacti with treelike proportions. Some of the resident saguaro on these slopes, and they seem to favor the sunny south-facing sides, grow fifty feet high. They assume fantastic, humanlike shapes, each a work of art surpassing anything by Praxiteles or Calder.

All the while my eyes are fixed on the heights. The deep blue sky is set in the jagged gaps and broken gulfs of Mount Ajo like pieces of turquoise. The crag is quite beautiful in its desolation. As with all things in nature, the mountain assumes a more formidable aspect as it is neared. Somewhere up there is an unmaintained trail, a pathway more familiar to the hooves of desert bighorn sheep than to the feet of a human.

Onward, into the heights, the road now turning back toward the south, making its leisurely way to the trailhead at the base of the next canyon.

All around, mountains as steep as falling rain dwarf,

Saguaro forest, Saguaro National Park, Arizona.

Hedgehog cactus, Joshua Tree National Park, California.

Chain-fruit cholla and Ajo Mountains, Organ Pipe Cactus National Monument, Arizona.

even mock, anything human. These are massive structures, the foundations of the earth heaved upward, crystallized rocks almost wholly defiant to erosion, and I am beginning to realize this will be a tough pull, not so much because of the heat, but because of the vertical nature of the terrain.

As predicted, the road shortly becomes terrible. I press on and finally the trailhead comes into view. My day pack full of water, I happily set off on the trail.

And it is a precipitous trail, almost immediately set at an angle of fifty or sixty degrees, something guaranteed to help you shed a few pounds, even if you don't need to. The trail, soon a ghost of a path, leads upward, through the canyon, into the heights. Everywhere, the plants of the Sonoran Desert show off their spring blossoms—the scarlet of teddy-bear cholla, the pink of hedgehog cactus, the red of barrel cactus. The saguaro and organ pipe won't blossom until late May or early June—they are the last, and the most lovely, to arrive at the party. Tiger swallowtails flutter, zebratail lizards dart, and energetic cactus wrens chatter from the palo verde trees.

Cactus forest in Ajo Mountains,
Organ Pipe Cactus National Monument, Arizona.

Up and over a ridge, sweating now profusely, I climb. This hike, it occurs to me, would be ill-considered on a 115-degree day in July, perhaps even fatal. On the far side of the ridge the trail drops unexpectedly into an expansive grassy basin—Bull Pasture—completely enclosed by impassable rock walls. It is a natural pasture, one of the better I've seen in the desert provinces, although a farmer from Georgia, where it rains nearly every day, would laugh at something as sparse as Bull Pasture being called prime grazing land.

Fortunately, the grass these days supports only what it was intended to: desert bighorn sheep and whitetail deer.

Crossing the basin, I come upon several pools of water, or *tinajas*, gathered in the eroded rock. Here is something more valuable in these parts than gold. At night these watering holes become as busy as an isolated bar next to a dry county. Among the rocks and rubble at the far side of Bull Pasture, I make an unpleasant discovery: there is no indication of a formal trail. From here on, travel will be by line of sight and gut instinct only. This is where the journey becomes interesting; if you fall, you may not be found until your children are grandparents, if then.

Cautiously, I begin the arduous, and exciting, part of the ascent.

The major challenge here is navigating the thick stands of teddy-bear cholla. This is a diabolical cactus, each plant comprised of hundreds of small joints literally bristling with barbed spines. These little pads easily detach from the mother plant and then attach themselves to whatever wanders by. In this way the primitive plant propagates itself. The problem is these miniature pincushions are difficult—

extremely so—to remove.

One false move, and I'll be covered with them, a walking cholla cactus, awash in blood, tingling with pain.

However, captured by the spell of the mountain, the excitement of my first encounter with a new country, and the lure of the panoramic view from the heights, I press on, using a dead agave stalk as both a walking stick and cholla deflector.

Gradually the annoying cactus zone is left behind. We enter—my walking stick and I—a sort of transitional area. The Ajos receive more rain than the lowlands, and as a consequence the vegetation up higher is different. There

Mexican poppies and cane chollas,
Organ Pipe Cactus National Monument, Arizona.

Utah agave, Grand Wash Cliffs Wilderness, Arizona.

Saguaro silhouettes, Saguaro National Park, Arizona.

Arva Valley, Saguaro National Park, Arizona.

Saguaro forest on Rincon Mountain, Saguaro National Park, Arizona.

are oak trees on the slopes, each with a litter of acorns beneath, and junipers, and much more agave than down lower.

The agave is a remarkable organism. Similar to a yucca in appearance, each plant produces a rigid stalk as tall as a javelin. The Indians obtained both food and fiber from the agave. In places, as I climb, there are whole forests of them.

After an hour and a half of scrambling and sweating I take a short break and prepare myself for the final assault. The loyal agave stalk is discarded. I briefly take in the view—but only for a moment, as it will be much better from the top.

Onward and upward, through the rocks, sometimes backtracking and trying an alternative route, pausing at times to catch my breath, always alert for rattlesnakes, never making the mistake of sitting down (as I probably won't rise for half an hour), ignoring the protestations of my quadriceps and that small blister forming at the side of the big toe on the left foot.

Higher now, the great peak soaring but within reach.

In places there are actual woods, with flocks of chickadees and groves of junipers and even a few thin patches of shade. The heights have the feel of mountain lion country, and every so often I glance behind, though I am armed only with the mighty pen.

False summits, several of them, and finally a staggering out on what must be the top. I scan the horizon for 360 degrees and confirm that, yes, I have reached the top of Mount Ajo.

The first order of business is to sit down—more like collapse—and take a restorative drink of water.

The view, as I had suspected, is tremendous. Sixty miles to the south is the Gulf of California: blue, sparkling water that beckons the tired desert traveler in ways that are difficult to describe. There is something about the sea. John Steinbeck knew about the sea, and especially about this one. He and his best friend, Ed Ricketts, a marine biologist from Monterey, took a boat to the Gulf and returned with a valuable collection. Steinbeck wrote a little-known, though excellent, book about the adventure, entitled *The Sea of Cortez*. Later, other distinguished naturalists visited that fabled desert by the sea: Joseph Wood Krutch, Ed Abbey, Ann Zwinger, and, lately, Sir Douglas Peacock. The Sonoran Desert of Arizona is, of course, the northernmost extension of that much larger subtropical desert to the south.

Closer to home is the International Boundary, just beyond the border station at Lukeville. By line of sight, the border is about fifteen miles away. The actual boundary is readily discernible because a Mexican highway runs parallel to the southern edge of Organ Pipe Cactus National Monument.

Not wholly in view is Quitoboquito Springs, a fifteen-acre oasis on the far side of the Puerto Blanco Mountains. Quitoboquito is the only wetland in the 330,000 acres of Organ Pipe Cactus National Monument. During the days of the El Camino del Diablo, or "Devil's Highway,"

Streambed in saguaro forest,
Saguaro National Park, Arizona.

Quitoboquito was a life-saving rest stop on the way to the Pacific. South from Mount Ajo is Diaz Peak, named for a conquistador who explored this country in the sixteenth century. Due west is Kino Peak, named for Father Kino, a pioneering Spanish missionary. Hard to believe Europeans were here—on this wild land in front of me—when Shakespeare was still in grammar school.

Turning to the east, I gaze out across the Tohono O'Odham Indian Reservation, the homeland of the Papago nation. It is a sprawling sun-baked province, with scattered mountains rising here and there like islands. Here are villages and placenames from another language, another culture: Kom Vo, Vamori, Pan Tak, Gu Vo, Ko Vaya. Here are a people who still practice the old ways, of planting melons and corn, and hunting the deer, and listening to the tales of Coyote and Raven. Here are also a people with an array of social and economic problems, one of which is overgrazing (an effect noticeable on the lower slopes of the Ajo).

Looking around the top of Mount Ajo I spot a metal

canister—a summit registry—and examine the contents. On the worn weathered pages are the names and messages of climbers from around the country and the world. Variously the inscriptions curse the "sickening" heat, marvel at the "freak" snow, or mention seeing bighorns on the way up. One couple drew a circle around a smiling face, which pretty much says it all. I add my name, the date, and something about letting the peace of the mountaintops reign on earth.

The sun is settling lower in the west and I turn to leave, but then pause.

One always searches for something to carry away from a summit. Once, on a mountain in northern Colorado, I came upon the carcass of a golden eagle. A few years later, I carried away the sun-bleached skull of a fourteen-year-old bighorn. And of course there was the time I discovered a 10,000-year-old Native American vision-quest site in Rocky Mountain National Park. I have spent much time in the western peaks, wandering around, looking for whatever treasures and treats persistent curiosity and random chance might reveal. Sometimes you find nothing. In fact, most times you find nothing. But about once

every decade, hiking steadily each summer, you happen upon the unexpected. Something to write about in the journal, something to reflect upon during the long nights of winter, when the streets are drifted with snow and the world has shrunk to a light table and a Muddy Waters tape.

The older I become the less inclined I am to search for *things*, in the sense of material objects, on these wilderness treks, and the more interested I have become in establishing facts, distinguishing subtle but significant differences, identifying truths, finding connections, apprehending patterns.

Moses climbed a mountain in the Sinai desert and returned with ten principles to live by. Whether from a divine encounter or not is impossible to determine, perhaps even irrelevant. What we do know is that, after a period of reflection, he descended from the arid heights with a set of truths that have endured for thirty-three centuries.

Over the years I have often thought we should add an eleventh. On Ajo Mountain, in the dying rays of the April sun, I consider one way to phrase it: "Thou shalt not harm the earth, or any other world on which you live."

Brittlebush and owl clover in Puerto Blanco Mountains, Organ Pipe Cactus National Monument, Arizona.

CHAPTER THREE

It seemed a more fitting abode for fiends, than any living thing that belongs to our world. During our passage across it, we saw not a single bird, nor the track of any quadruped, or in fact any thing that had life...This very extensive plain, the Sahara of California, runs north and south, and is bounded on each side by high barren mountains, some of which are covered with perpetual snow.

We [eventually] travelled up a creek about three miles, and killed a deer, which much delighted our two Indian guides. At this point we encamped for the night. Here [there were] an abundance of palm trees and live oaks, and considerable mescal.

—James O. Pattie
Personal Narrative (1831)

Colorado Desert

LIFE ON THE ROCKS

Let us say that for some reason—a job, a family, a familiar routine—you have spent the entire winter, or perhaps several, in a far northern city. A place like Caribou, Maine, or Moose Jaw, Saskatchewan, or that outpost I know so well, Fairbanks, Alaska. These are all fine places during the fishing season, and offer world-class blueberry picking in the fall, but lose much of their allure once the lakes and rivers freeze. You have risen every morning for six months to concrete gray clouds and arctic cold. Now it is late March. Despite the fact that the vernal equinox

Above: Teddybear cholla, Anza-Borrego Desert State Park, California.
Right: Mojave yuccas, Anza-Borrego Desert State Park, California.

Ocotillos in Coyote Canyon, Anza-Borrego Desert State Park, California.

Colorado Desert

LIFE ON THE ROCKS

has come and gone, snow has drifted over the driveway for the third time this week.

You look at the calender. You suddenly decide to pack the essential camping gear, drive to the airport, and catch a series of flights to Los Angeles. You arrive in the middle of the night and drive east through the labyrinth of highways with no one else on the road but newspaper delivery trucks and escort service limousines.

At Corona you turn south on the Interstate—as empty at 4 a.m. as it is crowded at 4 p.m.—and follow it to Temecula, where you take an old state route east into the countryside. The drive has so far consumed the better

Evening primrose,
Valley of Fire State Park, Nevada.

part of two hours, so vast is the City of Angels. It is raining lightly now, a weak front pushing over the Santa Ana Mountains. On either side of the road the orange groves are blossoming and you smell the flowers and realize once again that there is no sweeter fragrance in the world. Even though it is raining you drive with the window down. The scent is powerful, overwhelming, intoxicating and you wonder why anyone, least of all yourself, would live in any other place. After awhile you see black space and stars among the clouds—closer to the desert now—and somewhere on a peak to the south you can be sure the astronomers at the Palomar observatory are focusing the giant lens

Desert gold, Death Valley National Park, California.

Chollas in Pinto Basin, Joshua Tree National Park, California.

on some beautiful mystery.

The road climbs up over the San Felipe Hills, winding through the chaparral of the Los Coyotes Indian Reservation, and then, at the head of a series of dry brush canyons, it widens suddenly to a panoramic overlook and you pull over. Just then the sun is rising, and you gaze out with wonder and appreciation at the Colorado Desert, stretching away east to the Salton Sea, and beyond that to the Colorado River and Arizona, and then south a hundred miles into Old Mexico. You are certain of one thing—that some people have secret meetings and surprise memos, therapists and weekly groups, and other people have places like the desert. Quite suddenly that other world, the impoverished one that threatened to diminish the imagination and spirit, the one you wisely left behind for now, has ceased to exist, and you have rediscovered the freedom without which there can be, properly speaking, no life.

Some experts claim the Colorado Desert does not exist. They say it is merely the farthest western province of

Badlands at Font's Point,
Anza-Borrego Desert State Park, California.

the Sonoran Desert, or a southern adjunct to the Mojave. Others—the majority—disagree, and make the contrary argument, that the fauna and flora west of the Colorado River and south of the Chuckwalla Mountains are unique enough to merit designation as a separate desert region. Having seen all three, I agree with the latter position. The Colorado Desert is substantially different from the Mojave, to the north, or the Sonoran, to the east. For one thing, the Colorado is a much lower and drier desert than the Mojave, and lacks the Joshua trees, Mojave yuccas and other distinctive highland species. For another, it does not support the arboreal cacti of the Sonoran. You only find the saguaro and organ pipe once you cross the Colorado River, at Blythe or Yuma, and even then they are far from robust.

Think of these three deserts as three sisters, each lovely and charming in its own way, but each pleasantly different from the other, in terms of character, mood, and physical appearance.

The Colorado has this further distinction: It is the

smallest desert in the United States, coinciding roughly with the eastern half of San Diego County (for a total area north of the border of around 6,000 square miles). In Mexico the Colorado Desert, like both the Sonoran and the Chihuahuan deserts, is substantially larger, extending south through Baja California for a distance of some 600 miles, to the vicinity of Isla Angel de la Guarda. Only a small, tantalizing portion is found in the United States. With 500,000 square miles of desert in the United States, the Colorado is a desert that—with more extensive desert provinces nearby—could easily be overlooked.

But that would be a mistake.

Why?

First of all is the trail up Borrego Canyon, which is just down the hill from the panoramic overlook mentioned earlier. Borrego Canyon is part of Anza-Borrego State Park, which at 600,000 acres is the second largest state park in the coterminous United States (Adirondack the largest). It was formed, like so many of our desert parks, back in the 1930s when the Great Depression brought land values tumbling down. Borrego Canyon holds one of the most popular trails in southern California. The internationally renowned trail begins at the base of Indian Head Peak, just west of the quiet retirement town of Borrego Springs. Near the trailhead is an artificial pool—in which state biologists raise endangered desert pupfish.

Just past the pond is a wild overgrown patch of beavertail cactus which, on the day I visited, was literally covered with magenta blossoms that would put the best flowers of a championship rose tournament to shame. The unusual blue-gray pads of the cactus made the scene even more visually striking. Farther up the trail, the real wildflower show began, as the desert was awash in the cheerful yellow blossoms of the brittlebush and the "burning-bush" red blooms of the ocotillo.

Beavertail cactus and fan palms, Anza-Borrego Desert State Park, California.

Dried playa designs, Death Valley National Park, California

Teddybear cholla, Plomosa Mountains, Arizona.

My favorite was the barrel cactus. Each stout green keg—swollen with stored water—was tipped with a gaudy crown of red flowers.

And round the myriad flowers were industrious bumblebees, fluttering desert swallowtails, shiny black phainopeplas and iridescent green and red hummingbirds.

Half a mile farther on, the trail angled up and among some large rocks. Dug into one flat boulder were a pair of shallow rounded depressions, or *morteros*, and a long grinding slick, or *metate*. Here the Cahuilla Indians ground their yearly crop of mesquite seeds. How many centuries would it take to wear a groove in a rock four inches deep?

More than a few, I would think.

It being spring, Palm Canyon Creek ran full with water and in places there were some impressive waterfalls. I paused at the largest—which had an eight-foot drop—and watched. The cold water was compressed between two immense boulders, the stream jetting into open space, the rainbow-prismed mist, the roil and rush of the pool below, the green mesquite crowding the bank, heavy with

Desert senna, chollas, and ocotillos in Terra Blanca Mountains, Anza-Borrego Desert State Park, California.

Southwest Palm Grove,
Anza-Borrego Desert State Park, California.

spring buds, the stones and pebbles of the creekbed gleaming through the clarity of the water, the high rugged desert ridges above, and over it all, the brilliant wash of desert sunlight.

The creek would be dry in two weeks, running only in the event of a particularly powerful summer thunderstorm.

I pressed on.

Scattered here and there were creosote bushes—nondescript half-dead-looking bushes that live in soils and conditions where no other plant would exist. I've seen them in the dry washes of Arches National Park in eastern Utah and I've walked among them in Organ Pipe Cactus National Monument just a few yards from the Mexican border. Although people often speak of the bristlecone pine as being the oldest-living plant in the world, the creosote, in point of fact, owns that distinction. Not far from Borrego Canyon are creosote plants that scientists have determined are more than 17,000 years old.

Ahead, palm trees came into view.

Saltbush skeletons and sand dunes at Mesquite Flat, Death Valley National Park, California.

Colorado Desert

A bit of fast walking and I closed the final half mile to the first palm grove, one of two dozen in Anza-Borrego. These were the California fan palm, the only palm native to the western United States. It was a fine oasis, lush and green.

Coyote droppings near the trail indicated the local clan had been eating a largely vegetarian diet—animal prey would be scarce in such a canyon.

Climbing a sizable rock in the oasis, I scanned the surrounding hills for sign of desert bighorn sheep, but found none. If the local sheep were anything like their cousins, the Rocky Mountain bighorns, they would only come to water in the hours of dawn or dusk. The Peninsular bighorn sheep, as they are known, are the rarest bighorn subspecies on the continent. There are only about 500 left in the United States, and about 300 of them live within the protected confines of Anza-Borrego. When Captain Juan Bautista de Anza, the pioneering explorer, passed through in 1775, the Peninsular bighorns were much more numerous. Hence the canyon's name, which means sheep in Spanish.

Another fine place in the Colorado Desert, and one not far from Borrego Canyon, is Font's Point, which provides a detailed view of the Borrego Badlands. First of all, the glare

Alluvial playa and desert gold,
Death Valley National Park, California.

Badlands below Font's Point, Anza-Borrego Desert State Park, California.

Pressure ridges in salt pan at Devils Speedway, Death Valley National Park, California.

is stunning. You are gazing out at a hundred square miles of sun-blasted chaos—a wrinkled, tortured, grotesque and utterly ravaged landscape. Here, ancient deposits of mud and clay have been deeply eroded by the elements. Flash floods have scoured out V-shaped gorges. Sharp ridges have been cut into side-ridges and then the side-ridges have been further dissected as if by some mad artist into bizarre shapes of intricate complexity. No need to visit Badlands National Monument or Death Valley National Park—at Font's Point you've seen them both.

On the Fourth of July you can expect the thermometer to go over 100 degrees Fahrenheit shortly after sunrise, with temperatures considerably higher later in the day.

The scene from the overlook is, simply put, like something from Dante's *Inferno*. There is life, and there is anti-life. The Borrego Badlands is of the second category.

One of the few plants in these Badlands is the hardy creosote bush, which secretes a poison in its roots that kills any other plant, even its own kind. Similarly, the fauna are limited to the most basic organisms, creatures such as the

Creosote bush, Death Valley National Park, California.

fire ant, which survives by living in underground bunkers, and its nemesis, the giant hairy desert scorpion, which emerges after dark with those razor-sharp pincers and that menacing dangling stinger and that multipart mouth like something from an Edgar Allen Poe nightmare. If you are going to write an epic poem, and want to write about hell, Font's Point is the place to go for inspiration.

The Borrego Badlands does have one redeeming virtue—it contains a wealth of fossils. Most date back a million or two years, when the area was a Mesopotamia of streams and lakes. Paleontologists—often laboring in hellish temperatures—have unearthed the mineralized skeletons of mastodons, camels, extinct horses, sabertooth cats, and some sort of a meat-eating bird that had a wingspan of sixteen feet.

One is almost glad that such a dragon-bird is no longer patrolling the lonely backcountry trails of southern California.

Extinction, such as we see in the fossils of the Borrego Badlands, is a natural part of life on earth. What

North Algodones Dunes Wilderness, California.

Desert holly, Death Valley National Park, California.

has happened in our century—the loss of whole animal and plant nations—is not. The effects of this widespread disaster are seen even in the best-protected regions of the Colorado Desert, areas such as Anza-Borrego State Park. Besides the pupfish and Peninsular Bighorn Sheep, other endangered species in and around Anza-Borrego include the southern rubber boa, desert tortoise, barefoot banded gecko, Coachella Valley fringe-toed lizard, Yuma clapper rail, elf owl, gilded northern flicker, Gila woodpecker, and Arizona bell's vireo.

If nothing else, Anza-Borrego State Park and other sanctuaries like it are the modern-day equivalent of the biblical ark. A rising flood of humanity threatens to forever change the earth. Our only hope is in places like Anza-Borrego, in safeguarding them and in setting aside more areas like them. How well we do this may determine whether a distant posterity either curses or praises our tenure on Earth.

In the end, the Colorado Desert is more than a place to relax and recreate, to indulge the desires and pursue the idle whim. It is a place to embrace a larger and more comprehensive world, and to acknowledge the responsibilities that come with freedom. The Greeks believed, in one of their familiar paradoxes, that the more responsibilities you assume, the freer you become.

One of the lessons of this or any desert is that we must not leave it behind when we depart. We must do what we can to preserve that which has been so kind and generous to us. The desert, after all, has given us something more than a few days away from that *other* world. It has restored our understanding and our faith. The least we can do, as did the medieval knights of old, is to become sworn defenders of that which has saved us.

Vallecito Mountains,
Anza-Borrego Desert State Park, California.

CHAPTER FOUR

We departed the next day, and traversed a ridge seven leagues in width. The stones on it are of scoria and iron. At night we arrived at many houses situated on the banks of a very beautiful river. The masters of them came half way on the trail to meet us, carrying their children on their backs. They gave us many little bags of pearl, and of pounded antimony, with which they rub the face. They gave us many beads, and many blankets of cowhide [buffalo robes], and they loaded all that accompanied us with some of everything they had.

—Alvar Nuñez Cabeza de Vaca
The Relation of Alvar Nuñez Cabeza de Vaca
(Seville, Spain; 1542)

Chihuahuan Desert

A COUNTRY WITH NO ROADS

The Chihuahuan Desert was first seen by a European in 1529. In that year, there were no European settlements—none at all—on either coast of North America.

In the heart of that American Southwest, a thirty-five-year-old man named Alvar Nuñez Cabeza de Vaca was slowly making his way toward the place where the sun sets each night. With him were two other Spaniards, Castillo and Dorantes, and an Arab named Estevan. Originally crew members of a vessel shipwrecked on the Texas Gulf Coast, Cabeza de Vaca and his companions were lost in

Above: Ernst Tinaja, Big Bend National Park, Texas.
Right: Rhyolite blocks on summit of Emory Peak, Big Bend National Park, Texas.

the ultimate sense of the word. All de Vaca had was the knowledge that somewhere west of the Gulf of Mexico, where the de Narváez expedition had officially disappeared, was the northern frontier of the Spanish colony that Hernando Cortez had founded.

That, and faith in God.

And so he proceeded west, day after day, month after month, across what is now Texas, New Mexico, and northern Mexico—the heart of the Chihuahuan Desert. De Vaca and his companions maintained this ostensibly hopeless quest for eight years until, finally, after a Quixotic journey of several thousand miles, they were—in one of the most unlikely events recorded in

Ponderosa pines and pinnacles in Echo Park,
Chiricahua National Monument, Arizona.

history—reunited with their countrymen. Such is the indefatigable nature of the human spirit, that it will accomplish feats that even the boldest imagination would consider impossible.

The important thing for us to know here is that de Vaca wrote a book about his experiences, which is, among other things, the most readable American narrative of the sixteenth century. In that volume, the author provides many fascinating details about the Chihuahuan Desert, as it was in the beginning. The desert was, preeminently, a country with no roads. There were trails leading from village to village, most of the time, but nothing resembling the paved highways that

El Capitan and Delaware Basin from summit of Guadalupe Peak, Guadalupe Mountains National Park, Texas.

Ponderosa pines on McCarty's Lava Flow, El Malpais National Monument, New Mexico.

Prickly pear cactus and Mule Ear Peaks, Big Bend National Park, Texas.

had crisscrossed Spain, Italy, and the rest of the Mediterranean areas since Roman days.

After many years on the desert, he came to know as well as the natives the broad green pads of the prickly pear cactus, and the month when the fruit became edible, and how the nuts of the pinyon pine could make a life-saving meal, and that the yucca root produced a kind of soap. He was familiar with the red blossoms of the ocotillo in the spring, when they hung like a benediction over the desert, and at midday in the summer he had seen the mountains detach themselves from the earth and float on heat waves, and in the winter he had heard the Mexican wolves howl the moon up from the ridge behind the campfire.

The Chihuahuan Desert was the first desert I came to know on a regular basis, during my college years.

Each spring break, as I drove south on the interstate into the heart of the New Mexico brightness, I found a dry land, a windswept, empty realm of antelope and prairie dogs—but it was not the desert, not yet. In the distance there were mesas dark with ponderosa, and the cores of

Prickly pear cactus blossoms,
Saguaro National Park, Arizona.

Yuccas and gypsum dunes,
White Sands National Monument, New Mexico.

extinct volcanoes, and the occasional ranch house and windmill. Over everything was spread a parched wheatlike mantle of grama grass. On and on I drove, through the silence and the solitude.

Eventually, south of Ancho, the country changed. Quite suddenly, the prairie grasses disappeared. Replacing them were creosote bush, snakeweed, mesquite, and the tall, distinctive agave. Now I was in the Chihuahuan Desert, and I would lie down to sleep beneath the stars.

To sleep on the floor of the desert is to know the peace of Sophocles' unborn.

The facts about the Chihuahuan Desert, as I eventually learned, are not always what might be expected. For one thing, only about ten percent of the desert is in the United States (southern Texas and New Mexico). Ninety percent of the desert is in the Mexican province of Chihuahua, and extends nearly to the cities of Durango and Monterey—a distance of some 800 miles.

Overall, the Chihuahuan Desert can best be described as a desiccated plateau between two mountain ranges, the

Paperflowers, Big Bend National Park, Texas.

Chihuahuan Desert

A COUNTRY WITH NO ROADS

Sierra Madre Occidental and the Sierra Madre Oriental. These parallel mountains are of such a size as to intercept any weather that might otherwise bring moisture to the arid lands. Because so much of the desert is in Mexico, less is known—biologically and archaeologically—of the Chihuahuan Desert than other North American deserts. But one interesting fact is that the streams and rivers of the Chihuahuan Desert flow eastward, into the Gulf of Mexico and, eventually, the Atlantic Ocean. The watercourses of all other North American deserts discharge into the Pacific Ocean.

Of the three major national parks in the Chihuahuan Desert—Big Bend,

Terlingua Creek below Mesa de Anguila,
Big Bend National Park, Texas.

Carlsbad Caverns, and White Sands—it is likely that Cabeza de Vaca only passed through the first, Big Bend. If one studies his narrative and observes that most of the villages he described were near a great river flowing from the west, there can be little doubt but that he walked through this area.

Big Bend protects both the uplands and lowlands along a wide bend of the Rio Grande River. At 708,221 acres, Big Bend is the second largest park east of the Rockies (Everglades is the first). It is classic Chihuahuan Desert country—except for the centrally located Chisos Mountains. From a distance, the park is dominated by this rugged isolated

Gypsum dunes, White Sands National Monument, New Mexico.

Yucca leaves and gypsum sand, White Sands National Monument, New Mexico.

Bladderpod on sandbar in Rio Grande, Big Bend National Park, Texas.

massif of 6,000- and 7,000-foot peaks, all darkly covered with a relict forest of Douglas fir, aspen, ponderosa pine. The tops of those peaks, looking out over Old Mexico, afford some of the finest views in the national park system.

Like several national parks in the West, Big Bend owes its existence to a man-made disaster—the Dust Bowl of the 1930s. So badly overgrazed and eroded was this sunburned parcel of south Texas, that no one among the ranching community wanted it anymore. Thus was Big Bend born in 1944. Three years after its formation, Ansel Adams motored out from San Francisco in his beloved "Woody" to investigate. While in Big Bend he com-

Rio Grande in Santa Elena Canyon,
Big Bend National Park, Texas.

posed two of his best-known images—"Santa Elena Canyon" and "Sand Bar, Rio Grande River." Few other individuals have done so much to heighten public appreciation for the desert.

The Santa Elena Canyon is today one of the prime attractions of the park. Few desert canyons are as dramatic. The canyon walls rise as much as 1,500 feet above the river. In days gone by there were jaguars here, and Mexican wolves. In days gone by.

White Sands National Monument, which protects a 176,000-acre basin of pure white gyspum dunes, is located in the northernmost lobe of the Chihuahuan Desert.

Recently, White Sands National

Chisos Mountains, Big Bend National Park, Texas.

Scattered volcanic rocks on ash hills, Big Bend National Park, Texas.

Monument has found itself in the center of an intense environmental controversy. In June of 1995, the U.S. Fish and Wildlife Service announced a plan to restore the Mexican wolf—one of the world's most critically endangered mammals—to the area.

To restore the wolf to this remote part of southern New Mexico would, to my way of thinking, go a long way to erase some of the gross insults our culture has perpetrated upon the Chihuahuan Desert. The Mexican wolf was on the desert before the ships of Columbus set sail in 1492, before Cabeza de Vaca wrecked his boat on the Texas Gulf Coast, before Coronado set forth on his expedition. In another age, with different values, the wolves were exterminated from American soil, though they survived a bit longer in Mexico (now gone there as well).

It seems to me the Mexican wolf has much to teach the modern industrial world about survival: about the importance of hard work, tradition, loyalty to place, shared labor, and love of family. These are the stern old values and are the virtues first abandoned in times of plenty. Above all, the wolf teaches tolerance, and it is on tolerance that the foundations of a democratic society finally rest.

Lost Mine Peak and Toll Mountain from summit of Emory Peak, Big Bend National Park, Texas.

CHAPTER FIVE

On the nineteenth day we crossed the Great American Desert—forty memorable miles of bottomless sand, into which the coach wheels sunk from six inches to a foot. We worked our passage most of the way across. That is to say, we got out and walked. It was a dreary pull and a long and thirsty one, for we had no water. From one extremity of this desert to the other, the road was white with the bones of oxen and horses. It would hardly be an exaggeration to say that we could have walked the forty miles and set our feet on a bone at every step!

— Mark Twain
Roughing It (1871)

Great Basin Desert

A REPUBLIC OF SAGE

The Great Basin Desert is three things: our largest desert, our northernmost desert, and our most underloved desert. It is for most people that empty quarter that sprawls from Las Vegas to Reno to Salt Lake City. In fact, the Great Basin Desert is much larger than that, covering over 200,000 square miles in parts of seven states—California, Nevada, Oregon, Utah, Colorado, Wyoming, and Idaho. All with less than the population of New Jersey.

Above: Paintbrush and pinyon-juniper debris, Great Basin National Park, Nevada.
Right: Limber pines on Wheeler Peak, Great Basin National Park, Nevada.

Penstemon and pinyon pinecones, Great Basin National Park, Nevada.

Great Basin Desert

A REPUBLIC OF SAGE

Few visitors venture down the dirt back roads and investigate long-standing rumors of lost wildflower valleys, solitary mountain ranges, and hidden ravines of rare beauty. For most, the Great Basin Desert is an endless foreboding landscape of far-away horizons and shimmering heat waves, a forgotten badlands best crossed at night and under the stars.

For many years I was among those who mistakenly regarded the Great Basin Desert with less enthusiasm than the other deserts. The Great Basin lacks the massive natural bridges and free-standing arches, the magical vistas, the oasis palm groves, the finely sculpted Alexander Calder cacti, the

Bristlecone pine roots in quartzite talus, Great Basin National Park, Nevada.

bottomless dark canyons of the other North American deserts. The Great Basin is the geographic equivalent of the neatly dressed, plain-faced soul who sits patiently in the corner but is not asked to dance.

Why vanish into that lonesome country, I would say, when I can spend a week among the painted rock cities of Canyonlands? Subsequently, at different seasons and in subtle ways, I learned that the Great Basin, like the neatly dressed, plain-faced soul in the metaphor, has considerable virtues. For one thing, the campgrounds at Canyonlands may be overflowing each Easter, but in eastern Nevada, you, and you alone, can roam a piece of land

Ribs and couloirs on Wheeler Peak, Great Basin National Park, Nevada.

Bristlecone pine, Ancient Bristlecone Pine Forest, White Mountains, California.

larger than the kingdom of Alfred the Great.

The Great Basin Desert is impressively big in the atlas, but it assumes an even greater stature when we set out on foot. Our exploration begins along a fugitive byway in the extreme northwestern corner of Colorado, about sixty miles south of Rock Springs, Wyoming, and twenty miles east of the Utah state line. This is what might be called, for lack of a better phrase, the middle of nowhere. The land has the long, gentle lines of all ancient grounds. It is not difficult to imagine that this country was once at the bottom of the sea. Distant red sandstone cliffs, formerly Cretaceous reefs, are the bright red of fire coral. In their heights are scattered groves of pinyon and juniper. Among those trees are the shaded, secret places where mountain lions wait like vampires for the sun to go down and golden eagles carry vigorously protesting prairie dogs for lunch.

Elsewhere the country is the color of old broken pottery—the claybank gray of big-leafed sage, the faded green of rabbitbrush, the sunbleached white of dead Indian rice

Pinyon-juniper woodland in Diamond Mountains, Nevada.

grass. It is late September, and low clouds are scudding by fast. To the east are high mountains where it snows every month of the year. The wind is steady, Dust Bowl dry and strong enough to take possession of a loose baseball hat. The locals will tell you that on the floor of the Great Basin Desert, it is always windy.

The Great Basin is not only dry and windy, it is also surprisingly cold for several months each winter. This northern desert is a place where newborn lambs often freeze to death and range cattle have been known to shed frostbitten ears. For that reason, cactus are scarce. The sole cactus we find on our walk this morning is prickly pear, extending those familiar, flat green-spined pads and desiccated purple fruits. I have seen prickly pear near timberline and I have found them on the shores of alkaline lakes. They are by far the most adaptable of our native cacti. All they need is some sunlight, a patch of soil, and a sprinkling of water a few times each year. They are the plant kingdom's version of a philosopher beyond all earthly suffering. There are in these parts no ocotillo, no cholla, hedgehog, or beavertail cacti, and certainly nothing resembling an organ pipe or saguaro—too unfriendly a clime for those succulent southern sun-loving species.

What we mostly see—sprinkled lightly from the top of the hills to the bottom of the valleys—is big-leafed sage, the most widespread plant in the Great Basin. But sage was not always so plentiful. As cattle and sheep devoured the wheat grass, the sage took over. Today there are more sage than people in the Great Basin. Unfortunately, there is not much human use for sage, except in potpourris and scented candle wax. The sage, along with the greasewood and saltbush, thrive in the Great Basin partly because of the soil—they are among the few plants that can tolerate it. Grab a handful. The soil in which they live is not dark loam, rich humus, or even poor sand. It is, rather, a fine, crumbling powder with high concentrations of salt. Many of the resident Great Basin plants, a group known as halophytes, have developed the ability to secrete that salt through glands in the leaves. The salts are then washed off by the rains.

Down close to the ground we come upon one of the most distinguishing features of the Great Basin Desert—mounds of harvester ants. What is most amazing about these miniature pyramids, the largest of which are perhaps eighteen inches tall, is that the industrious occupants have removed every piece of vegetation in a circle ranging to ten feet around their mound. And I do mean *every* piece of vegetation. The ground is vacuumed, completely devoid of any clutter or debris. There is not so much as one fallen bird feather, one errant wind-blown twig, or one carcass of one dead moth. Like the prairie dog and other burrowing animals, the harvester ant actually helps the soil of the Great Basin Desert by aerating it, recycling nutrients, and improving water availability.

A little farther on, past another half dozen or so harvester ant mounds, we come to the pelvis and sacrum and lumbar

Eroded bentonite hills, Cathedral Gorge State Park, Nevada.

Rabbitbrush and granite boulders below eastern Sierra Nevada, California.

Western juniper on Devils Homestead Flow, Lava Beds National Monument, California.

vertebrae of a pronghorn antelope or mule deer. The ants have picked them clean. The sun has done the rest. We examine them—who can resist a skeleton? Here are the remains of an animal that was born, lived, and died on the Great Basin Desert. Never left it. Never knew anything but it. If ever there were an authority on the desert, the owner of these bones was it. If only they could talk, could tell us about the long winter nights with Orion wheeling and the coyotes singing, and the coming of the first purple pasque-flowers in the spring and the fawns delivered among the yucca, and the fall breeding battles as the days grew short and the does came into heat. A further look produces recognition of some fractured ribs, a scapula, and a well-gnawed femur. Nothing else remains. The skull, the horns or antlers, the organs, and the hide are nowhere to be seen. Coyote scat is nearby, filled with the remains of a mouse. No clues there. Perhaps the animal died of old age. Perhaps a mountain lion.

Only the wind knows, and it is not telling.

One animal definitely absent is the black-footed

Petrified wood,
Granite Range, Nevada.

Bristlecone pines at Wheeler Peak Bristlecone Pine Grove, Great Basin National Park, Nevada.

ferret. Although it once ranged across this corner of the Great Basin Desert, it is today the second most critically endangered mammal in the United States.

We have reached the top of an escarpment now and enjoy an expansive view. To the southwest, fifteen miles as the crow flies, are the Gates of Ladore. Through those towering rock portals flows the Green River. Beyond is Dinosaur National Monument, known regionally as Jurassic Park.

Today the upland area in which we walk has been designated as the Vermillion Basin Wilderness Study Area. Like so much of the Great Basin Desert, the Vermillion valley and its environs are managed by the Bureau of Land Management. At 88,340 acres—over 130 square miles—Vermillion Basin includes saltbush desert, pinyon-juniper woodlands, brilliantly colored badlands, ancient fossil beds, sandstone canyons, prehistoric Indian petroglyphs and various wild plateaus and mesas.

We hike a bit farther in, reaching an overlook to the eerie red and orange badlands to the north, and then turn

Aspen and mountain mahogany in Lamoille Canyon, Ruby Mountains Scenic Area, Nevada.

back to the end of the road where this hike began. It is re-assuring to know the Vermillion Basin is still there, lost and largely unaccounted for, another one of this nation's priceless treasures safely forgotten in the enormous vault that is the American West. There is nothing there of special interest to any but painters and poets. Prospectors would be better advised to search for revelations than radium in this cold northern desert—the former have greater power in this world.

The finest writer to visit the Great Basin was not John Wesley Powell or John Fremont, but Mark Twain. In July of 1861, after two unpleasant weeks in the Confederate Army, Samuel Clemens and his brother Orion decided it might be a good idea to head West. Orion had somehow gotten himself appointed "Secretary to the Governor of the Nevada Territory" and the plan was to have Sam serve as secretary to the secretary. Somewhere along the way Sam Clemens changed his name to Mark Twain and switched his vocation

from journeyman ne'er-do-well to apprentice world writer. His subsequent record of the trip, *Roughing It*, constitutes the finest prose ever written about the Great Basin Desert. Even 135 years later, his vivid descriptions of the desert resonate with truth and sparkle with felicity. Salt Lake City "lies on the edge of a level plain as broad as the State of Connecticut...and is suggestive of a child's toy village reposing under the majestic protection of the Chinese wall." Twain's word-picture of the Great Salt Lake desert, which includes the well-known Bonneville salt flats, is just as insightful and eloquent:

> Imagine a vast, waveless ocean stricken dead and turned to ashes; imagine this solemn waste tufted with ash-dusted sagebrushes; imagine the lifeless silence and solitude that belong to such a place; imagine a coach, creeping like a bug through the midst of this shoreless level,

Mud formations in bentonite, Cathedral Gorge State Park, Nevada.

Tufa formations at Mono Lake, Mono Basin National Forest Scenic Area, California.

and sending up tumbled volumes of dust as if it were a bug that went by steam; imagine this aching monotony of toiling and plowing kept up hour and after hour, and the shore still as far away as ever, apparently...

Eventually, on the far side of the Great Basin Desert, the exhausted, back-sore, sunburned, homesick, incredulous brothers from Missouri reached their destination of Carson City. Here they found the gambling saloons, bawdy houses, banks, mining claim offices, and various state and federal buildings that collectively comprised the capital of the newly established Nevada Territory:

Visibly our new home was a desert, walled in by barren, snow-clad mountains. There was no vegetation but the endless sagebrush and greasewood. All nature was gray with it. We were plowing through great deeps of powdery alkali dust that rose in

Dried playa on Black Rock Desert, Nevada.

thick clouds and floated across the plain like smoke from a burning house. We were coated with it like millers—we and the sagebrush and other scenery were all one monotonous color... We moved in the midst of solitude, silence and desolation. Every twenty steps we passed the skeleton of some dead beast of burden, with its dust-coated skin stretched tightly over its empty ribs. Frequently a solemn raven sat upon the skull or the hips and contemplated the passing coach with meditative serenity.

Coming from the "waterworld" to the east, where the muddy mother river is a mile wide and summer rains nourish corn to the height of a barn door, the brothers—like the rest of America—were clearly shocked to discover a realm where in a good year there may be only nine or ten inches of precipitation. Like all deserts, the Great Basin is most easily defined by what it lacks. It is an incredible fact that

Sunset over Simpson Park Mountains, Nevada.

Pilot Peak and pool at Little Salt Spring, Nevada.

Great Basin Desert
A REPUBLIC OF SAGE

in the century since *Roughing It* was published, no other writer has written so powerfully of the Great Basin Desert.

We as a people have treated the Great Basin Desert with at best indifference and at worst contempt. Of all the North American deserts, the Great Basin has suffered the most, from nuclear testing to overgrazing to urban sprawl. The desert, though, will remain. It will quietly undergo the beautiful changes that all things with eternal life experience. I take some comfort in that. All that we have done and created will one day disappear from this universe, but the Great Basin will remain.

Think about that the next time you drive across the Great Basin, and perhaps mistake, as people sometimes do, the wide-open spaces for emptiness.

Salt playa on Black Rock Desert, Nevada.

CHAPTER SIX

They made the Sun of fire with a rainbow around it, and put the Turquoise man into it as its spirit, the Moon was made of ice, with the White Shell man as its spirit. They put the Fall and Winter in the West and North, and the Spring and Summer in the South and East; the month of October was claimed by Coyote, it is half summer and half winter and called the changing month.

—Navajo Creation Myth

Painted Desert

THE LAND THROUGH WHICH THE RIVER RUNS

If you have watched the movie *She Wore a Yellow Ribbon*, or *The Greatest Story Ever Told*, or *Butch Cassidy and the Sundance Kid*, you have been transported, for a few hours, to the Colorado Plateau. If you have opened a magazine and admired the colorful and bizarre rock formations in a car advertisement, you have glimpsed the Colorado Plateau. If you have owned a mountain bike and wondered where the best mountain biking is, you have sooner or later become acquainted with the Colorado Plateau. If you have taken up the sport of river rafting, you have at

Above: Navajo Falls in Havasu Canyon, Colorado Plateau, Arizona.
Right: Tumbleweeds in a water-carved sandstone room, Colorado Plateau, Arizona.

some time during the first summer heard tantalizing rumors, amazing descriptions, impossible accounts, wistful campfire reminiscences of the Colorado Plateau. If you have wondered where the pollen-yellow, energy-rich uranium comes from that powers those glittering spiderlike probes we periodically dispatch on five-year missions to Jupiter, Saturn, and beyond, you have learned about the Colorado Plateau.

The Colorado Plateau, also known as the Painted Desert or the Slickrock Country, is unlike any other part of North America or, for that matter, the world. Here is the greatest collection of natural rock arches and bridges—in Arches National Park alone there are 1,500 of them. Here are more national parks and monuments than in any other similar-size region of the country, and some of the largest roadless areas remaining in the Lower 48. Here are canyons as deep as four Empire State Buildings stacked on top of each other, and as wide from rim to rim as Manhattan Island is long. Here are meteor impact craters into which a sprawling Midwestern mill town could easily be made to disappear, and exposed dinosaur tracks as plain as the day on which they were made, and the empty stone villages—hundreds of them—of vanished civilizations that flourished while Europe languished in the Dark Ages.

Delicate Arch,
Arches National Park, Utah.

Entrada formations in Fiery Furnace, Arches National Park, Utah.

Balanced Rock and the Windows Section before La Sal Mountains, Arches National Park, Utah.

Totem Pole and Yei-Bi-Chei formations, Monument Valley, Arizona.

Geologically, the region is defined by what the Colorado River and its tributaries have done, over millions of years, to a vast sedimentary rock formation. What they have done—water on rock, day by day, century after century—is to make, to create, to *sculpt* a myriad of canyons, reefs, mesas, spires, pinnacles, bridges, free-standing fins, dissected volcanic cores, deeply eroded lava flows, and delicately balanced rocks.

It is an enormous outdoor museum, a living gallery in which those Old World masters—earth, wind, water, and fire—continually practice, and refine, their craft.

There are many spectacular views of the Colorado: the panoramas from Bright Angel Overlook on the Grand Canyon, from the two-lane blacktop across Monument Valley, from the slickrock rim above the White House Ruins in Canyon de Chelly. Every Western American artist of stature from Alfred Bierdstadt to Ansel Adams has made the pilgrimage to one or more of these places, and been inspired. My favorite, among those accessible by road, is Grandview Point in Canyonlands National Park.

Grand Canyon National Park, Arizona.

Supai cliffs at Toroweap above the Colorado River,
Grand Canyon National Park, Arizona.

One of the best times of the year for Grandview Point is early March, after the short days of winter have passed, but before the legions of tourists have arrived to embrace the desert spring. Late afternoon provides the most favorable light. A sprinkling of fast-moving clouds helps to scatter a changeless, ever-changing pattern of brightness and darkness over the landscape. You stand at the edge of the cliff. Your foot dislodges a pebble and in counting the seconds until it strikes the White Rim you determine that the cliff is at least 900 feet from top to bottom. Impressive. You step back a little. Especially if it is gusty, which it will most likely be. You are, in a manner of speaking, standing several inches from the rooftop ledge of an eighty-story building. If a cliff swallow swoops by, chasing a sulphur butterfly in a downdraft, and you happen to make the mistake of watching the bird pursue its prey in the great gulf below the cliff edge, you will definitely become a little dizzy. If you are lucky, that is all that will happen. If you have a camera, you will now step back a respectful interval and mount the device securely on a sturdy tripod.

Vishnu Temple and Freya Castle, Grand Canyon National Park, Arizona.

Now you are faced with a decision. Due east for thirty miles the view is superb, but the peaks of the La Sal Mountains behind Moab are obscured by a snowstorm. Toward the west, you have the Henry Mountains, rising like an island seventy miles away, but because it is afternoon the light has gone flat on them and they appear only in silhouette. They would be best about two hours after sunrise, or held up against a fiery Turner sunset. The best prospect at this hour is directly south, toward the Abajo Mountains, which are about sixty miles from Grandview Point as the cliff swallow flies. There appears to be a minor rainstorm in progress in the western foothills of the Abajo. Otherwise they are perfectly clear, and the towering white cumulus clouds and single dark column of falling rain will make the back range more interesting. You begin to frame the composition, and then, stopping to consider the foreground, you pause. The complexity of the scene between Grandview Point and the Abajo Mountain has now made its presence fully known to you.

How to describe this wonderland? It is a scene from another age, another planet, another universe. For one thing it is ninety-five-percent rock. Plants are practically nonexistent. Animals are also conspicuously absent, as they almost always are, in desert regions during the day. For another, the various rocks are a veritable catalog of terrestrial geology. There are rock formations—especially over toward the Maze in the far southeast—shaped like elaborate turrets. Elsewhere there are rocks—as in the region just this side of Sixshooter Peak—that seem part of a fractal landscape, a scene derived from an equation that organizes chaos in strange, random patterns. There are territories—directly below Grandview Point—that resemble the utterly barren, foreboding landscapes of that untrekked desert world, Mars. And Grandview Point itself, as seen from below, presents the appearance of a vast, Homeric rampart looming over a denuded wasteland.

Mount Hayden, Grand Canyon National Park, Arizona.

Colorado River and canyonlands, Dead Horse Point State Park, Utah.

And through it all flows that greatest of rivers in the American West, the Colorado. I have stood at the headwaters of the Colorado River in Rocky Mountain National Park, at a place called Kawuneechee Valley, and watched the speckled brook trout dart among the polished stones, and listened to the bull elk bugle in the aspen groves, and I have jumped the miniature channel and spent the day on higher slopes where the river is indistinguishable from the snowfields whose dying give it birth. Farther downstream, near Yuma, Arizona, I have walked beside the Colorado seventy miles from its outlet on the Gulf of California. Nowhere along its entire 1,450-mile length is the Colorado River more beautiful, more muscular, more powerful than in prospect from the Grandview Overlook in Canyonlands National Park.

Nowhere.

Why?

Because here the river is at its maturity, in full career, halfway between birth and death, as yet undammed in any significant way, still running wild and free through a country it began rearranging when creatures the size of railroad

Mesa Arch, Canyonlands National Park, Utah.

cars still roamed the earth. In the Grand Canyon you peer into an abyss. It is a vision of time more than anything else. At Grandview Point you consider a landscape that stretches a hundred miles from horizon to horizon, a distance so immense one nearly detects the curvature of the Earth. Grandview is a revelation of space. Everything you see—except the three fault-block mountain ranges—has felt the touch of the river or one of its hardworking tributaries.

It is not enough, of course, to stand on the overlook and peer into this, or any, country. One must, or at least I must, walk into it, touch it, smell it, even spill some blood on it, courtesy of a yucca spine or cactus barb. A good place to begin, in coming to terms with the Colorado Plateau, is Grand Gulch Primitive Area, a 54-mile-long canyon that drains from Cedar Mesa south of the Abajo Mountains into the San Juan River, which in turn empties into the Colorado River. Here the Bureau of Land Management has established a 400,000-acre "archaeological wilderness" that preserves the cliff dwellings and kivas of the Old People, the Anasazi.

Painted Desert

THE LAND THROUGH WHICH THE RIVER RUNS

The trail to Grand Gulch begins on a little-traveled highway south of Natural Bridges National Monument, about halfway to Muley Point (another splendid overlook, this time of the famous "Goosenecks" of the San Juan). On the day I arrived at the Gulch it was early March and there was the feel of spring in the air. In other parts of the land, people struggled with blizzards and subfreezing temperatures and cabin fever. Here was a different season, entirely. I found the old familiar trail—all trails are old and familiar, even new ones—and followed it through a sunny pinyon and juniper woodland into the upper portals of the canyon. Between the parallel walls of rock the air was immediately still, and there was the intimate quiet of a contained space—a country church, a college library, an empty courtroom.

Out of the breeze, the sun had some genuine heat to it, and there was fresh grass on the south-facing slopes. And in the side pools of the intermittent stream at the bottom of the canyon there were bright green mats of algae. I paused by a shallow pool along the way, knelt for a moment and lifted a few strands of algae to observe a swarm of tadpoles and water beetles.

The trail soon entered a cottonwood grove, and I picked up a peeled walking stick someone had dropped on the way out and took it with me on

Colorado River and Inner Gorge,
Grand Canyon National Park, Arizona.

Washer Woman Arch and Monster Tower, Canyonlands National Park, Utah.

Water-sculpted sandstone canyon, Colorado Plateau, Arizona.

Weathered sandstone layers, San Rafael Desert, Utah.

the way in. It would be useful later, pushing sluggish black-tailed rattlesnakes off the trail and probing into dark crevices while climbing around on the rocks.

Instantly, on passing through the wilderness gate, there was that feeling of exhilaration, of liberation, that always attends one's departure from the settled country and return to pristine nature.

Steadily the canyon walls deepened, from twenty or thirty feet to more than a hundred feet, in the space of a mile. Looking up, I saw white Cedar Mesa sandstone, unclimbable overhangs, the formidable palisades of the netherworld. At times the trail disappeared, and travel involved climbing up and over and around and literally through (via cracks) elephant-size boulders. At other times the trail was wide enough to comfortably accommodate a pregnant draft horse, with flood-washed sand underfoot to ease the walk.

Spring progressively became more evident—the swollen pussy willows, the partially leafed cottonwoods and oaks, the budding yuccas and prickly pear cactus, the

Boxelder in sandstone alcove,
Capitol Reef National Park, Utah.

Virgin River upstream of The Pulpit,
Zion National Park, Utah.

singing sage sparrows, the chanting canyon frogs, the first sprouts of what would in a few weeks become the blossoms of red Indian paintbrush, desert sunflower, blue penstemon, white peppergrass, wild plum.

The most significant surprise in the first four miles was the aspen trees, scattered here and there in the deep shaded alcoves, elegant white-barked visitors from the snowy mountains that had somehow found their way here, in the depths of the lower desert. Their size indicated that they had been rooted in place for decades. Like so much of nature, they would not have seemed possible had I not seen them with my own eyes.

The second unexpected discovery was the many waterfalls cascading over polished, green slickrock into deep clear pools. The largest dropped a good thirty feet into a wide basin encircled with a natural garden of moss, fern, and wild rose more perfect than anything a gardener could create.

Another interesting feature was the huge perched boulders. One specimen was so prodigious it required a

Balanced Rock, Valley of the Gods, Utah.

Painted Desert

THE LAND THROUGH WHICH THE RIVER RUNS

photograph. No one would have believed my description—like a three-quarter-ton truck poised on its right front headlight. Judging from the "desert varnish" on the rock, the boulder had been there for a very long time. Somewhere I read that geologists consider balanced rocks to be a natural indicator of seismic stability. If that is the case, the Colorado Plateau must be one of the most geologically stable regions on the planet.

Nothing moves at the bottom of those 600-foot canyons but the water and the water striders, the butterflies and the deer, the reflections of the clouds and constellations.

Eventually Grand Gulch met with a side stream and it was there, on a grassy bench, that I came upon the extensive remnants of an Anasazi village. The houses, granaries, and kivas were not on the flats, of course, where they maintained their fields, but were perched high in the rocks, in the manner of cliff swallow nests or honeybee hives. The highest structures could only have been reached by a rope ladder of fifty feet or so, for there was nothing but naked, featureless rock between the rock shelf and the ground. In those secluded retreats the resident Anasazi had stored the precious seeds of maize, melons, beans, and sunflowers in sealed stone vessels, safe from rodents and birds. Other dwellings—the bulk of them—were clustered in an overhang that formed a shallow cave. The cave faced southeast, where it would catch the sun early in the winter months, but would be protected from direct sunlight in the hot summer months. The whole affair was about the size of a grade-school gymnasium.

I hiked up to the cave and spent quite a bit of time exploring the stone village. The place was actively superintended by an irregular platoon of collared lizards. They were *everywhere*, staring at you, following you, in their own quiet way letting you know you were not welcome to stay longer than a short while.

Pine boughs and Queen Victoria formation, Bryce Canyon National Park, Utah.

Juniper boughs and West Mitten Butte, Monument Valley, Arizona.

Cottonwoods, maples, and Gambel oaks below a sandstone wall, Zion National Park, Utah.

What struck me most about the ruin was this: despite the fact that the tracks of visitors indicated the place was not unknown, undisturbed artifacts were visible in great quantity. There were, in no particular order, scattered pieces of ancient painted pottery; arrowheads and other sharpened stone tools; grinding stones; piles of discarded 900-year-old cobs of cultivated corn; the remnants of pipes, reed baskets, and in one case what appeared to be the sole of a child's straw sandal. Modern visitors had respected the sanctity of the place, and their restraint restored some of my faith in human nature.

In the end, the Colorado Plateau country is many things. It is a three-

Claret cup cactus,
Capitol Reef National Park, Utah.

week-old black-tailed rattlesnake sunbathing on a 300-year-old brachiopod fossil. It is a mountain lion drinking with her kittens from a pothole at the base of Navajo Mountain. It is a popular hiking trail at the bottom of a gulch a thousand feet deep and ten feet wide, and the indestructible core of a volcano that darkened the skies five million years ago, and a standing rock arch longer than a football field. It is a raft plunging uncontrollably into a twenty-foot standing wave at the bottom of Cataract Canyon, the helpless occupants literally holding on for their lives, the unsecured cargo spilling out, the oars now useless as the river holds them for a moment as if in idle curiosity, then hurls them sideways into the next rapids where the waves are considerably larger.

It is finally and less dramatically, a juniper growing from a crack as wide as your ankle in a piece of slickrock behind an obscure campground in southeastern Utah. Whenever I think of the human endeavor as less than ideal, I think of that juniper growing in the middle of the huge rock amphitheater, a good thirty feet from the nearest soil, an organism that had no choice in where the wind or the bird on the wing left its seed. And yet it dutifully rooted there in the middle of a rock, and made the best of it, and persists in that enterprise, of helping to split a rock, still.

Each time I visit the Colorado Plateau I hike up to that ancient juniper and pay my respects. It has, after all, taught me much of patience and persistence. There it remains, cheerfully growing and sometimes even producing a crop of seeds, all the while being baked in summer and frozen in winter. How it finds moisture and nourishment in that fissure is one of the unsolved mysteries of my experience.

That, to me, is the essence of the slickrock country, of organisms flourishing in some of the hardest country known to man or woman on this earth. In such acts, perhaps, can be found the ultimate nature of the universe, and, indeed, perhaps even the elusive meaning of life itself.

Rim above Silent City,
Bryce Canyon National Park, Utah.

There is a relation between the hours of our life and the centuries of time.... The hours should be instructed by the ages, and the ages explained by the hours.

—Ralph Waldo Emerson
Journals

Afterword

Not long ago I visited the Kelso Dunes in newly formed Mojave National Preserve. Here, at the end of a gravel road on the far side of the Old Dad Mountains, I came face to face with what the national debt would look like if every grain of sand was one dollar. Forty-five square miles of sand. To the south and west were jagged volcanic peaks, the likes of which prospectors dream about. To the north, though not wholly in view, was a landscape of uneroded lava flows known as the Devil's Playground. To the east were the Providence Mountains, a heavy solid range with timber on top and dusted with snow. Rumor had it desert bighorn sheep lived there.

Above: Petroglyphs on a sandstone block, Valley of Fire State Park, Nevada.
Right: Dumont Sand Dunes, Amargosa Canyon Dumont Dunes Natural Area, California.

Afterword

In the center was a sea of sand. And sea is a carefully chosen noun, for the sand was sculpted in massive waves. It was a sea that moved with refined slowness, the wind-driven waves forever about to crest and crash. If I listened carefully I could hear the sand blowing, a soft, pleasant murmur. The dunes were all that remained, a ranger had told me that morning, of previous desert mountains eroded by the elements. Such would be the fate, she assured me, of the Rockies, the Sierras, the Himalayas. As I climbed the tallest one—which was the height of a seventy-story building—the sand underfoot made a peculiar hollow sound, presumably caused by the rubbing together of the polished grains of rose quartz. It was a low rumble, a distant thunder, the dead mountain remembering the stature and power it once had. This venerable patriarch—ground to its essentials by the ages—had presided over a vast span of North American history. The coming and going of the dinosaurs, epic migrations, dramatic conflicts, spectacular events we will never know about.

Much to think about, climbing seventy stories in the shifting sands.

At the top of the dune I sat down. It was hot in the heights but still slightly cooler than at the base. All along the crest, amazingly, grew the yellow upright flowers of desert primrose and clustered purple mats of desert sand verbena. Most people would give such plants little heed, but each one was a miracle, the culmination of a billion years of evolution, the triumph of persistence over adversity. Here, in a square yard, was more life than on all the sand dunes of Mars. We could spend eternity exploring this universe, and likely find nothing so fantastic as a yellow primrose on Mojave sand.

I looked around, took my bearings. Twenty miles to the south, over a wide pass in the Old Dad Mountains, was Route 66. I had driven over the road earlier on my way to the Kelso Dunes, stopped and taken a photograph of the now-forgotten

Afterword

thoroughfare. A considerable amount of twentieth-century American history journeyed down that highway. The refugees of the Dust Bowl in the 1930s knew Route 66 well. They had little choice when the Great Plains were turned into a desert as a result of human greed, grotesque agricultural practices, and egregious drought. Forty million unemployed, one in four farms foreclosed, the California valleys beckoning like Arcady. In *The Grapes of Wrath*, John Steinbeck described the Mojave of the Joads' era as "the terrible desert, where the distance shimmers and the black cinder mountains hang unbearably in the distance."

Terrible?

Only to those who do not recall the lessons of history, who fail to learn the principles of nature.

Emerson was right. The ages should inform the hours. We need places like Mojave National Preserve, places to go and sit outside time for a while. Places to remember what is important and what is not. Places to absorb the silence and the tranquility. Ages will pass, and much of what we see will change, yet nothing that matters will change. These sanctuaries will remain.

There will be other worlds, other places for the human race to explore. There will be other deserts. But there is only one Earth, only one set of American deserts.

Posterity will return to this world, tired from their travels in the lonely gulfs between the stars. They will be grateful that people in our distant age reached out in love to save these lands.

Further Reading

Abbey, Edward. *Abbey's Road.* New York: Dutton, 1979.

Abbey, Edward. *Desert Solitaire.* New York: McGraw-Hill, 1968; Tucson: University of Arizona Press, 1988.

Abbey, Edward. *The Best of Edward Abbey.* San Francisco: Sierra Club, 1984.

Adams, Ansel. *Autobiography.* New York: Little Brown, 1985.

Alcock, John. *Sonoran Desert Spring.* Tucson: University of Arizona Press, 1994.

Austin, Mary. *The Land of Little Rain.* Boston: Houghton Mifflin, 1913.

Bourke, John Gregory. *On the Border with Crook.* New York: Scribner's, 1891; Lincoln: University of Nebraska Press, 1984.

Bowden, Charles. *Blue Desert.* Tucson: University of Arizona Press, 1986.

Bowden, Charles. *Frog Mountain Blues.* Tucson: University of Arizona Press, 1987.

Dobie, J. Frank. *Tongues of the Monte.* Austin: University of Texas Press, 1980.

Dutton, Clarence. *Report on the Geology of the High Plateaus of Utah.* Washington, D.C.: U.S. Government, 1880.

Fletcher, Colin. *The Man Who Walked Through Time.* New York: Knopf, 1968.

Goetzmann, William H. *Exploration and Empire: The Explorer and the Scientist in the Winning of the American West.* New York: Norton, 1967.

Howard, Oliver O. *My Life and Experiences Among our Hostile Indians.* Hartford: Worthington, 1907.

Krutch, Joseph. *The Desert Year.* New York: Viking, 1963.

Lopez, Barry. *Desert Notes.* New York: Scribner's, 1976.

Nabhan, Gary. *Gathering the Desert.* Tucson: University of Arizona Press, 1985.

Powell, John Wesley. *The Exploration of the Colorado River.* Washington, D.C.: U.S. Government, 1875.

Stegner, Wallace. *The American West as Living Space.* Ann Arbor: University of Michigan Press, 1987.

Trimble, Stephen. *The Sagebrush Ocean: A Natural History of the Great Basin Desert.* Reno: University of Nevada Press, 1991.

Twain, Mark. *Roughing It.* New York: The Century Company, 1872.

Van Dyke, John Charles. *The Grand Canyon of the Colorado.* New York: Scribner's, 1920.

Williams, Terry Tempest. *Refuge.* New York: Pantheon, 1991.

Zwinger, Ann. *Downcanyon.* Tucson: University of Arizona Press, 1995.

Zwinger, Ann. *Run, River, Run.* New York: Harper and Row, 1975.